Are you VUCA ready?

To contact the authors please write to:

Charles May at **charles@talentfactor.co.uk** or
Jayne May at **jayne@hroptions.co.uk**

www.vucaready.com

Second edition October 2014

Note to readers

We dedicate this book to you the reader but research[1] indicates that only a mere 10% or so of what you read in a book will be retained.

Thankfully this figure increases dramatically to around 75% when you put into practice what you have learned. Therefore when you move from being a reader to a doer and take time to complete the questions and activities, you are increasing your return on the investment by over 7 times.

If you use it to teach others immediately after you have read it, then your retention rate can be as high as 90% which is why we have made this a **work** book and not simply a **text** book.

Enjoy putting this to the test

Charles and Jayne May

---

[1] Statistics shown in Chapter Five

Contents

What on earth is VUCA? 8

From Volatility to Vision 27

From Uncertainty to Understanding 42

Activity

How do you learn?

We all learn in different ways. Imagine you received a new piece of technology that you have never used before:

What would you do?

1. Take it out of the box, switch it on and see how it works by intuition and experimenting.
2. Ask someone to show you.
3. Leave it in the box while you read the instructions and then follow them step by step.
4. "Google" how to use it.
5. Leave it in the box and ignore it, sticking with what you know until you have no choice but to use it.
6. None of the above.

What is your preferred style of learning and how can you experiment with new ways of learning outside your comfort zone?

Chapter One
What on earth is VUCA?

September 11, 2001 radically changed the way many viewed terrorism. No longer was the enemy contained in some foreign land, it was in our schools, offices and retail parks. People we grew up with, lived next to and worked with, could be engaged in terrorism right under our noses.

In 2014, radical Islamic group, Islamic State (IS) is reported to have recruited more than 12,000 foreign nationals from at least 81 countries, including 2500 from Western States in the past 3 years.

The term VUCA was invented in the US to describe this dramatic shift where Volatility, Uncertainty, Complexity and Ambiguity became the new norm reflecting the increasingly unstable and rapidly changing threats to security. VUCA was first used around ten years earlier by the US Army College "to prepare select military, civilian and international leaders for the responsibilities of strategic leadership".

Today, VUCA principles are not only embedded in the military but are used by many to describe the volatile and uncertain world we live in. We have always lived with change but the rate of change is getting faster and will continue to increase in the future; and that is what we mean by VUCA.

In business, Chief Executives who once had 2-3 years to make an impact are expected to transform organizations within months of arriving. In 2013, it was reported that US corporations were switching CEO's at the fastest pace in 5 years and required a much broader range of skills than in the past[2]. Successful leaders know they must integrate the business and people strategies to achieve sustainable competitive advantage and no longer see so-called "soft" skills as optional.

Public outcry against greed and mismanagement in banking and other financial institutions has reinforced the need for integrity and ethics as a core CEO trait.

An annual study[3] of CEO changes at the largest 2500 companies' worldwide recorded turnover of 14.4% in 2013, even higher in Brazil, Russia and India at 21.1%. Telecommunications was the most volatile place to work in terms of job security with CEO turnover at 22.1%.

It may be surprising to note that in spite of these changes, 80% of CEOs came from the same country as their company headquarters and 65% had no experience of working abroad. 3.6% of CEOs were female.

British born Linda Jackson is currently the first woman and non-French person ever to head up the car manufacturer Citroen, joining an elite group of only three women to become CEO of an international car manufacturer.

[2] Business Financial Post 26 November 2013

[3] Strategy &, 14th Annual Chief Executive Study 2012 (formally Booz and co.)

Activity

Imagine you are starting out in your career now. What would be your ideal job and why?

_____

Where do you want your future career to be?

1 year from now?

_____

3 years from now?

_____

5 years from now?

_____

More questions to consider

1. Is what you are doing today building for your future or are you simply existing?

_____

2. What changes do you want to make now to benefit you in years to come?

_____

3. Bearing in mind only 35% of CEOs have spent time operating outside their home country, would an overseas opportunity benefit your career?

_____

4. Looking at your own life, have you spent time living in another country and if so what impact did it have on you in terms of career and other opportunities?

_____

5. What are some of the paradoxes we live with today that do not make logical sense?

_____

6. Does expert knowledge have a shorter shelf life in your profession today compared with ten years ago?

_____

7. How do you keep up with developments specific to your profession?

_____

What does VUCA stand for?

The acronym VUCA describes four factors that together contribute to an unstable and rapidly changing world:

Volatility – the speed of change

The Boston Consultancy Group found that over the past 30 years, half of the most turbulent financial quarters in the US economy happened since 2002. The increasing rate of destabilization has thrown predictable cause and effect out and replaced it with a confusing range of responses that can often only be understood after the event.

Human behavior does not always follow logic as evidenced by observing public events where the flow of large numbers of people towards an exit can be made safer by the erection of barriers, dividing up the flow, which serves to speed up the evacuation. Scientists observing crowds assumed that barriers would slow people down but were surprised to find the opposite to be true.

Sadly we all know the dangers when something unexpected happens in a large mass of people and panic occurs. Within seconds calm order can turn to chaos and in the same way business markets can be thrown into confusion because of some seemingly minor event that can grow into consumer panic within a very short time such as a run on a bank.

On 24 March 2014 a rumor spread that the Jiangsu Sheyang Rural Commercial Bank in Yancheng, China turned down a cash withdrawal and therefore was in trouble. For three days customers queued at branches to take out their money while staff tried to calm them down by displaying large piles of cash behind windows in an attempt to reassure them.

On 1 October 2008 Pieter Lakeman appeared on TV telling customers of the Dutch bank DSB that it was in their personal and collective interest to take their money out of their accounts. Lakeman was protesting about the way the bank handled mortgage lending and accused DSB of being aggressive and claimed it was in the borrowers' interest if the bank went bust. Within 12 days that is exactly what happened as a direct result of his campaign. This is what we mean by **volatility.**

Disruptive technology that radically alters the way we do things on a global level is a major contribution to volatility. Take the cell phone. In 1973 Motorola produced the first hand held mobile phone and made a call on a brick-like item which weighed 1.1 kg. By 1983 they sold a version that took 10 hours to charge for 30 minutes of calls. By the early 1990s, text messaging was developed and some phones were down to 100 grams in weight.

At the start of the 21st century the first cell phone payment systems were operational and the demand for internet browsing increasing with the introduction of 3G. 4th generation technology optimized data and brought speed improvements with Smartphone technology that enabled streaming of audio media, reversing the trend for ever smaller phones. Today we have larger devices with screen sizes big enough to watch our favorite TV programs while ordering groceries, texting a friend and reading work emails without leaving our beds.

Questions

1. Give examples of disruptive innovations or technologies that have affected your life and state why:

_____

_____

_____

2. How did you embrace these changes?

_____

3. What would you do differently if you had your time again and these innovations were new today?

_____

4. What innovations are there in your experience today that could cause such a disruption?

_____

5. What are the next global disruptive innovations?

_____

_____

The invention of the printing press brought newspapers and books to the world on a massive scale changing forever global access to reading material. In 2013 the world's first 3D gun was made on a printer layering material to build solid objects. Hospitals are developing 3D printed artificial limbs and technologists are using off the shelf printing tools to create functional body parts including a bionic ear. Car manufacturers are experimenting with the same technology to make vehicle components.

What other sorts of applications can you imagine being printed using 3D technology in future?

What are the implications of this technology for traditional manufacturing businesses?

Henry Ford's lower priced Ford Model T car changed our mode of transport from horse-drawn carriage to motorized vehicles. Today we have the autonomous vehicle capable of sensing its environment and taking us from A to B without the need for a driver.

Will the driver-less car become the next disruptive innovation and if so how will it change our world?

Wikipedia brought collaboration and knowledge sharing to everyone with access to the internet, replacing the Encyclopedia Britannica in 2012 when they stopped printing after 244 years because people were prepared to contribute information for free. Google have now launched their eye glass computer with the objective of producing a mass-market hands-free computer worn on the face.

Will the google glass change the way we access information and knowledge?

Express courier and parcel services have enabled 24-hour internet shopping to deliver to customers worldwide with massive warehouses sorting millions of items every day, reducing trade on the high street and bringing items to our homes at the press of a button. In Australia drones are planned to be used to deliver textbooks in 2015 and Amazon are testing unmanned "Octocopters" to deliver packages up to 2.4kg within 30 minutes of an order being placed.

If automated drones replace delivery vans and postal services what opportunities and challenges would that bring?

Uncertainty – the lack of predictability

The lack of predictability in events and the unstable way we react to issues has increased in recent years. The Chinese have a proverb: to be uncertain is to be uncomfortable, but to be certain is ridiculous," suggesting this is nothing new but the rate of unpredictability has accelerated. Shock events such as 9/11 and natural phenomena such as tsunamis, earthquakes, floods and hurricanes seem to happen with increasing regularity.

Our news channels display war, violence and brutality on a daily basis. Prominent figures have been accused and in some cases found guilty of sexual misconduct at an alarming rate.

Formerly stable economies have fallen foul of volatile inflation rates, economic downturns, soaring unemployment and low growth causing currency devaluations and concerns over government borrowing.

Does the immediacy of media make natural disasters, economic downturns, violence and hardship appear more frequent compared with 100 years ago or have they actually increased?

What markets do you operate in and what sort of disaster recovery plans do you have in place, if any, to cope with these impacting on your organization?

How do you cope in a crisis?

Think of a time you had to respond in an emergency/crisis situation?

_____

How did you cope?

_____

If it happened again what if anything would you do differently?

_____

What sort of steps can you take now to better prepare you for turbulence ahead?

_____

Complexity – multiple choices and confusing chaos

The World has become more complicated.

In 2010, IBM held face to face interviews with 1500 CEOs who cited complexity as the most significant challenge facing them at that time and many seriously doubted their own ability to cope with rapidly escalating complexity.

Businesses state there are often numerous causes to explain a problem and several factors that may have added to the situation rather than one obvious cause. Added to that are random events which serve to change things in a way that is confusing to make sense of.

Many country borders have effectively become meaningless and globalization has enabled the emergence of China and India to interface with organizations across the globe allowing Western businesses to offshore things like call centers and manufacturing processes, opening up new opportunities for some and closing them down for others.

Technology has connected us to individuals and organizations globally. We can operate from home using Skype to talk to people across the world and LinkedIn to share expertise without the need for expensive office space.

Logically this increased access to technology should make things simpler yet few would suggest that has actually been the case. Data has become more confusing and information more complicated.

Question

Why is it that the divide between rich and poor is getting wider and deeper, yet the world is now "flat" in terms of opportunities being made much more accessible globally? Before if you lived in a community with poverty you had to move to an area with prospects, often another country to succeed. Technology advances and global offshoring have moved work to areas of intense poverty so why is it that the difference between rich and poor is getting bigger not smaller?

World Events since 2000

Since the start of the 21st Century a large number of events have impacted our lives. Here are some of them:

2000 Dot-com bubble
2001 9/11 Al-Qaeda attack in the US killing 3000
2001 The US and NATO forces invaded Afghanistan
2001 Gujarat earthquake in India killed around 20,000
2001 El Salvador mudslides, killing thousands
2003 Saddam Hussein was overthrown in Iraq
2003 War in Darfur began
2003 Mars Exploration rovers launched
2003 European heatwave killing 30,000 in the hot summer
2003 Bam earthquake in Iran killed over 26,000
2004 Hurricane Jeanne killed over 3000 in Haiti
2004 Asian Tsunami killed around 230,000
2005 Hurricane Katrina hit the US killing 1836 people
2005 Kashmir earthquake killing over 74,500

2006 Mumbai train bombings killing 209
2007 2010 financial crisis
2008 Barack Obama became President of the US
2008 DVD players replaced VCRs
2008 Recession in US cascaded into worldwide recession
2008 Cyclone Nagris killed over 100,000 in Myanmar
2008 Sichuan earthquake killed at least 70,000
2009 Bushfires across the state of Victoria, Australia
2009 L'Aquila earthquake in Italy killing 308 people
2003-2010 Emergence of China and India
2009 Influenza A (H1N1 strain) spread globally
2010 Haiti earthquake killed at least 230,000
2010 Chile earthquake
2010 Yushu earthquake in China and Tibet
2010 BP Gulf oil spill environmental disaster
2010 Iceland ash cloud from a volcano grounded flights
2011 Osama Bin Laden was killed
2011 Fukushima nuclear disaster in Japan
2011 Muammar Gaddafi was captured and killed in Libya
2011 Riots in the UK started in London and spread
2011 News of the World phone hacking scandal broke
2013 First baby cured of HIV virus in US
2013 Pope Benedict XV1 resigned & Pope Francis elected
2013 Nelson Mandela died
2013 War in Syria
2013 Edward Snowden spy allegations
2013 Typhoon Haiyan in the Philippines killed around 7000
2013 Coup in Egypt
2014 Malaysian airlines flight MH370 disappeared
2014 Iraq crisis
2014 IS and jihadist militants gain power in Syria
2014 Scotland voted against devolution
2014 What next?

Ambiguity – the potential to misread a situation

The world has become more ambiguous and we may struggle to grasp the significance of an event. Leaders removed from the source of a situation may form the wrong understanding and make decisions that do not reflect the reality of what is going on. Instead of two choices we may be faced with several and the real risk is to do nothing or to over-simplify and make decisions based on a false reality.

The increased rate of technology enables a company to offshore operations to the other side of the world but communication barriers mean organizations struggle with misinformation caused by differences in culture and interpretation, even when speaking the same common language.

Our veterans are dying out, the baby boomers are living longer, many Gen X are struggling to plan for retirement as pension funds disappear, our Gen Y Millennials are technology savvy and Gen Z are the first to grow up in a truly digital world. We need to be adept at appreciating the value of generational differences and looking at ways of leveraging opportunities to build bridges between them. We also need to work out how to support the growing numbers of older people in our societies.

Global education has been in a state of rapid transformation with an explosive growth in higher education worldwide. In 2008 a man with higher education could expect to earn 58% more than someone with no more than upper secondary education and in 2010 this figure rose to 59%[4]. In contrast the NEET[5] population across OECD countries was around 16% in 2010 leaving large numbers of 15-19 year olds without work or educational opportunities.

Question

Have opportunities for education increased or decreased in your experience and why?

The gap between rich and poor is getting bigger and is expected to continue this way unless we make decisions that reverse this trend. Secretary-General Ban Ki-moon told the United Nations assembly in 2013[6] of widening gaps between rich and poor that are "contrary to United Nations principles, with societies where hope and opportunity were scarce and were vulnerable to upheaval and conflict. Social and economic inequalities bred crime, disease and environmental degradation, as well as hampered economic growth. We live in a time of profound change and considerable uncertainty," he said, noting that successive global crises had shocked economies and brought severe distress to the world's poor and vulnerable.

[4] University World News 16 September 2012

[5] Not in employment, education or training

[6] General Assembly of the UN, Growing Gulf between rich and poor 8 July 2013

Ensure your intent is understood

We need to speak plainly to make sure others fully understand what we mean and not use jargon or terms that are not clear to others. Some enjoy using complex terminology to impress but in reality the best communicators are those that can adapt their message to the audience and be sure that others understand what they are talking about.

One day a pastor of a large church was asked by his youth group to do a talk on sex. He agreed and wrote down the appointment in his diary but instead of writing "Talk on sex" he decided to call it "Talk on sailing", embarrassed in case anyone saw his schedule.

A few days before the time the youth leader rang the pastor to confirm he was still OK for the talk. This time the Pastor's wife answered and said she would check his diary for the appointment.

Well said the perplexed Pastor's wife, viewing the appointment, I don't know what qualifies him to talk on that, he has only ever done it twice, the first time he felt sick and the second time it was so windy his hat blew off, she said to the rather confused youth leader.

A good communicator is as
stimulating as black coffee and
just as hard to sleep after
(Anne Morrow Lindberg)

Balanced communication

VUCA communicators will be balanced in the way they present information. They will not dumb-down their language to the lazy level of the "Tweet" or text message, nor will they elaborate using long words that many do not know. We will express ourselves properly and explain things so that everyone can understand our meaning.

> *Think like a wise man but*
> *communicate in the language*
> *of the people*
> *(William Butler Yeats)*

What next?

We need to be adept at making sense of the VUCA confusion and have a mindset able to adapt to its challenges, applying learning in every aspect of our lives. Gone are the days when we can study an MBA and be set up for a life in business. The VUCA world demands knowledge updated and skills honed daily.

At the June 2014 London Business School Global Summit on Leadership[7], Gary Hamel told the audience "Outdated management practices are leaving organizations ill-equipped to deal with the challenges of the 21st century, adding "there is nothing that has been more disruptive over the last couple of decades than technology. In that change most organizations have struggled to stay relevant," he said. "We are held hostage by an old management model. It has left us with organizations that are too incremental at the same time as innovation and passion drive performance," concluding that "the companies who will be the most successful are the ones who adapt their management practices more quickly than the rest."

To be VUCA competent, turning the challenges to opportunities, we need to recognize our lives are entwined and apply these principles to every facet of our professional, home and social lives.

We need turn VUCA challenges into VUCA competencies.

That means **Volatility into Vision, Uncertainty into Understanding, Complexity into Clarity, and Ambiguity into Agility**. That is what the rest of this workbook is about.

---

[7] Dr Gary Hamel, American leadership expert, founder of Strategos consulting firm.

Chapter Two

From Volatility to Vision

In the VUCA world situations we face will have many variables, some connected, some not. We will have volumes of data that can help to predict outcomes but only if we have the right information and can make sense of it. The phrase "Garbage in – garbage out" will describe the risk of taking data at face value and using it to make decisions.

There will be a demand on leaders in every part of life to be certain about which decision to take but there will be an increasing danger of over-simplifying and jumping to conclusions without proper analysis of facts. VUCA competent people will need to make sense of the chaos and volatility ahead of others if they want to play a key role in the future. We will all need to step back and see the whole picture, analyze it and reflect on what patterns emerge.

Business strategies will need to be holistic, bringing together long-term vision into a systematic description of what the business will do to realize the vision and a clearly defined plan of how to get there.

It is difficult to see the picture
when you are inside the frame
(R S Trapp)

Bringing light into a dark world

Alfredo Moser literally turned darkness into light when he invented the Moser lamp, an empty plastic water bottle filled with water and bleach[8] placed through a roof to reflect sunlight into the building underneath, as effective as a 40-60 watt light bulb. Moser the mechanic designed the no cost device to light up places during electricity blackouts in Brazil, in 2002, and the idea took off globally.

Myshelter foundation in the Philippines adopted the lamp in 2011 to bring daylight where people had lived in virtual darkness before and in Dhaka Bangladesh, businesses and families in shanty towns have benefitted immensely from the devices, preventing the dangerous alternative of tapping illegally into power supplies.

To make sense of our surroundings we need to see through the chaos, seeing the whole picture not just our own small part of it. Like the Moser lamp we need to bring innovation to all those who can benefit through communication and collaboration rather than it being the world's best secret.

Visionary ideas do not need to be all or nothing, permanent solutions, we need to keep reviewing them, making improvements as we go. Many ideas start as something else and it takes real vision to apply them in a new context.

Richard Jones was trying to make a meter to monitor power on battleships when a tension spring fell to the ground, bouncing around in an unusual pattern – with a bit of imagination he turned it into the Slinky children's toy.

---

[8] The bleach is to keep the water clear inside the bottle

John Hops was researching the effects of hypothermia using a radio frequency to restore body temperature. He discovered if the heart stopped due to excessive cooling his radio device started it again, resulting in the invention of the pacemaker.

Patsy Sherman was working on a project to develop a material that would not deteriorate when exposed to jet aviation fuels when some rubber mixture she was trying out dripped into her shoe. She noticed that when the rest of the shoe got dirty the one place where the substance fell stayed clean, inventing Scotchgard protector.

Life's cynics

A pessimist confronted with 2
bad choices, choses both
(Jewish quote)

Some people look at life as a long list of problems and decisions as unsolvable dilemmas, deciding to adopt the cynical cannot-do approach to life.

These people will mock those who want to improve situations and call you idealistic or worse when you share your vision for the future. For every encourager there are probably 2 pessimists who will tell you why it won't work and maybe they are right but I doubt Spencer Silver worried about that when his attempt to make strong adhesive failed as it stuck to objects but then peeled off- inventing the Post-it note.

Challenge the status quo

*Where you come from is not
nearly as important as where
you are going*

The world is full of rules, some written, others inferred, about what kind of education, background, gender, race and age we need to be to succeed. Rosa Parks didn't accept regulations referring to 'whites only' seats on buses. Richard Branson and Walt Disney didn't allow a lack of formal high school qualifications to stop them entering the business and film world. Mo Farah, born in Mogadishu, Somalia moved to London at the age of 8 where he struggled academically. A teacher identified his talent for running during football practice and encouraged him to try athletics; he didn't let his past stop him from becoming one of the world's best runners.

*If you think you are too small to
make a difference – try going to
bed with a mosquito in your
room
(Dame Anita Roddick)*

To be a visionary we need to recognize that the day to day challenges may be more appealing but if we spend the majority of our time focusing on today's problems we will not be leading people, organizations or family members to be VUCA competent in the future.

Coaching volatility to vision

> *Give a man a fish and feed him
> for a day. Teach him to fish and
> you feed him for a lifetime
> (Chinese proverb)*

It is so easy to fall into the trap of spoon feeding people by doing things for them, but all we are doing is fuelling our need to control and at the same time preventing others from equipping themselves with skills for the future. Allowing people in any context to try things out for themselves, with encouragement and feedback, is the coaching style we need to adopt in every part of our lives whether it is in our home or work life.

A teenager will never learn to solve a complex homework question if we tell them the answer, a nervous employee won't learn to handle a difficult client if you take the call and the pilot will never be able to fly a plane unless you hand over the controls. We need to allow people around us to see problems as challenges that they will enjoy solving and take the time to guide them through new experiences until they become competent, giving them our time and having patience to see them do it for themselves.

Being a visionary

If we want to lead others forward in a VUCA world we need the skills to share a picture that enables others to see how to deliver new products and services for the future.

- To be a visionary, surround yourself with visionary people. There is no point in trying to be a visionary when everyone else is pulling against you. Find people who are like minded, positive thinkers with the mindset to be open to new ideas and spend time with them.
- Invest time in your own life vision. Where do you see yourself in 10, 20 or even 30 years? Imagine yourself on your deathbed looking back on your life. What would you want to reflect on?
- Be able and ready to explain your vision as an "elevator pitch" keeping it simple and easy to communicate in as few words as possible.
- Visit science events, design workshops and creative studios to learn new ways of doing things and think through how they could apply in your life.

Your Life Vision

No matter what our opinions are of what happens at the end of life it makes good sense to be fulfilled in this one.

There can be nothing as depressing as a life full of regrets and wasted opportunities. In the VUCA world we need more than ever to be clear on our purpose in life.

> *Big thinking*
> *precedes great*
> *achievement*
> *(Wilferd Peterson)*

Activity

1. Allocate undisturbed time to writing down your own life vision. This could be sat quietly in a room, a long walk, a favorite fishing spot; whatever works for you.

2. Imagine you are at the end of your life looking back.

3. What would you want to see? Draw a picture or write a story of the life you hope you will have had.

4. Imagine your funeral, what would you want people to say about you?

5. What changes do you need to make now to enable this story or picture to become reality?

6. What is stopping you from making these changes right now? Make a conscious choice to either remove the blockers or live with the consequences of not making the decision to change.

7. What goals & plans can you make now for the next 10 years to enable this to happen? Push solutions that will take you towards your life goals and avoid distractions that pull you backwards including negativity about your own situation.

8. Summarize your life vision so that it can be your "elevator pitch" – crisp and clear so that it can be communicated to another person in the time it takes to go from the ground to the fifth floor of a building. Write it somewhere you can see on a daily basis.

9. Share your vision with a trusted person and commit to 3 actions you will start now that will move you towards your life vision.

10. What 3 things do you need to stop doing that undermine your life vision?

11. Every day speak your "elevator" vision to yourself out loud (if possible) and stop at least once every day and ask yourself: Is what I am doing today taking me towards or away from my life vision?

12. First thing in the morning remind yourself of all the things you have to be thankful for.

Focus on the important

A well-known retailer spent large sums on security to catch shop lifters. They were quite successful in apprehending people who did not intend to pay. They also drilled into their customer service staff the need to protect company finances by examining the validity of customer returns, ensuring a proof of purchase before giving a refund.

A new store manager removed all shop security guards and replaced them with people to welcome customers into the store and guide them to products. He also put a new emphasis on controlling waste by ensuring goods about to reach their use by dates were discounted early and sold. All customer services staff were told to offer refunds on any purchase with or without a receipt for any reason and were trusted to make decisions without needing approval from a manager.

Guess what, profits went up because genuine customers enjoyed the smiling face at the entrance and knew that they didn't have to fight to get a refund on a purchase. Yes the shoplifting continued but the amount lost due to theft was far outweighed by the increase in customer satisfaction and the volumes saved by selling rather than throwing away produce. Before long the store manager was made Director of Customer Service for the whole organization and they rolled out his approach company wide.

Be a visionary and a strategist

We need to take our visions and put them into actions. There is no point in writing a wonderful vision down and then filing it. Set your direction and work out the steps you need to get there – in other words your strategy.

Keep revisiting the vision and make sure it still makes sense, update it if necessary and completely change it if you need to.

Everyone has setbacks, even the most successful entrepreneurs have challenges in life. Richard Branson described his school years as a nightmare. At 15 he left school to set up his own music magazine followed by a record store. At 20 he avoided paying taxes by pretending to export records abroad but instead selling them in England, got caught by Customs and Excise, narrowly avoided prison and ended up paying a fine of £60,000 equivalent to around £700,000 today. He wrote in his first autobiography that the lessons learnt including the shame of having to move back to his parents' house and a crash course in running a legitimate fast growing business to pay the fine within two years or go to jail, are what made him into the billionaire he is today.

Success is not final, failure is not fatal: it is the courage to continue that counts (Winston Churchill)

Don't focus so much on the horizon that you miss potholes in the road

Vision is important but we need to be aware of what is going on immediately around us. The daughter of the head of an organization had planned a surprise gift of a large painting for her parents to celebrate an important milestone. She arrived at the venue where a large party was being held to commemorate the occasion but as she arrived her father opened the car boot to take out some wellington boots which were next to the unwrapped painting. Knowing her father well, she told the guests that if he father was looking for boots he wouldn't have noticed the painting.

Don't be a visionary who is so focused on the future that you fail to take notice of what is happening around you. People could be screaming out to warn you of a threat but if you are not in tune with what is going on you could miss something vital. Listen properly to what others are saying and be prepared to suspend judgment to consider another viewpoint to make better decisions.

In 2010 it is rumored that one morning the rig operator of an oil platform was seen arguing with a senior BP official about the methods used to seal gas to stop it rising up the drill pipe. At 9.45pm that evening the same Deep Water oil platform caught fire and sank, killing eleven workers and causing the worst environmental disaster in history because seawater was being used to seal the pipe instead of a much more expensive lubricant.

A well respected University of Japan professor, Katsuhoko Ishibashi, warned Japanese officials that the country's nuclear power plants were at risk of serious damage or even melt-down because they had been built in earthquake zones and proposed more rigorous surveys but was ignored. On 11 March 2011 Fukushima Dilachi nuclear reactor was severely damaged by an earthquake that triggered a tsunami causing a level 7 disaster, the highest on the scale. "If Japan had faced up to the dangers earlier, we could have prevented Fukushima" said Ishibashi in May 2011.

Are you listening?

Activity

Carry out this listening exercise with another person. Ask the person to speak for 5 minutes on a subject of their choice, such as a recent vacation and listen to what they say. The rules are that you cannot speak other than to repeat back their last sentence as a prompt. At the end of 5 minutes repeat back everything you can remember then ask them to recall anything you missed. If you prefer to do this alone, listen to a webinar for 5 minutes and do the same. This will help you to improve listening ability and to concentrate properly on what the other person is saying.

How much of the 5 minutes did you recall? How could you improve your listening skills?

Cascading a vision

It is key that everyone working together on a project or in a business has the clarity about the purpose and direction.

Agree an "elevator pitch" summary of the vision for your organization, that can be explained in a few short sentences and get everyone in the organization to use it when they communicate to their teams, new employees, customers and potential new hires. They don't need to be word perfect but the meaning needs to stay the same.

Nothing endures but change
(Heraclitus 540 BC – 480 BC)

Turning volatility into vision

In simple terms it is about the ability to see opportunities that others miss. Listening intently to what is going on around and being able to articulate a clear vision that others want to be part of. Like the Moser lamp, it can be simplicity itself but the impact is amazing.

From vision to strategy

Every organization from the multi-national to the small business needs to translate vision into a comprehensive strategy that articulates long term intent so that the people involved know what is required and by when. The business plan will provide the specific details but it is the strategy that should be used to measure performance and be the checkpoint to see if what each employee is doing is adding value to the organization. Every action, decision and process needs to reflect the strategy and any activity that is not in line should be stopped. The benchmark is to check that everything is adding value to the strategy in terms of increased revenue, reducing cost, increasing output or improving the quality of its product or services. Anything else is superfluous to the strategic objectives of the organization.

The business strategy needs to incorporate the people strategy and be led by the CEO. If the senior leader is not clear that the people elements belong in the high level strategy then review how Enron became the largest bankrupt organization worldwide because of the actions of a number of their senior executives. More recent scandals in the financial world have all stemmed from human deception and mismanagement. Many employment issues wouldn't be problems at all if the business strategy clearly stated the expectations of each employee and how each person is expected to contribute to the overall strategy, together with the systems to ensure the right people are in the company.

When an organization integrates the HR and business strategy into one, people can see how their own performance builds the business and of course the reverse is true. Everyone has clarity about their contribution and can ask themselves if what they are doing is really adding value.

To be in this position the organization has to be culturally mature. Strong leaders will head up teams and there will be an adult-adult employment relationship. Innovation will be commonplace so that everyone will be encouraged or even expected to make improvements to processes and to suggest new ideas. The focus will be on performance improvement and learning from any mistakes rather than a blame culture.

Organizations with a culture of fear or "them and us", dividing managers and employees will no longer have the competitive advantage because companies who differentiate in terms of talent and commitment will move ahead. Business leaders are using terms such as the "war for talent" to describe what is simply getting the best value from your workforce and the only way of doing that is to have willingness and commitment on your side.

The head of customer services for a catering organization was frustrated by the poor quality of people he employed where standards of service were awful and absence levels high. As a training exercise he took his senior team to the finest restaurant in town where service was five star. Imagine the shock when he discovered one of his very own members of staff was working in the restaurant displaying exactly the qualities he strived to attain. It was a great illustration of how with the right leadership and performance standards the very same person was quite capable of delivering the service he required.

Chapter Three
From Uncertainty to
Understanding

Is knowledge power?

We may know the phrase "information is knowledge and knowledge is power", but how do we apply that in a world where each of us receives more information in a single day than our counterparts only one generation ago received in a year.

Senior managers of Fortune 1000 companies complained of six e-mails interrupting their work per hour in 1997. In 2013 it was estimated[9] that 507 billion emails were sent each day and of those around 81% were SPAM or viruses. Today's senior managers are getting closer to 200 emails per day; add to that phone calls, texts, tweets, video conferencing, skype & conference calls, face to face meetings, ad hoc conversations, Facebook messages, Linked In contacts, blogs and the odd piece of post!

How on earth can we make sense of this information overload? We need to find a way of understanding the data and turning it into meaningful knowledge.

---

[9] The Radicati Group Email statistics report 2009-13

Activity

For one day (or one week if you want to analyze this properly), keep a running total of all of the pieces of data and information you handle or communications you are involved in. Total up the different types of communication and ask yourself the following:

- Am I using the best tool available to send and receive that type of information?
- What information do I not need to see?
- When is face to face communication preferable?
- What ways can I be more effective in handling information?
- Ask people close to you to appraise your communication styles and get feedback on areas you can improve.

Be curious

Curiosity motivates exploration and a search for new knowledge. We are all born with it but sadly many of us are discouraged from asking questions and exploring new ways of doing things as we grow older and many adults are fearful of finding things out because they do not want to appear ignorant.

Many of us will stay quiet when we do not understand something instead of asking for clarification. If you don't understand – find out. Richard Branson didn't understand the difference between gross and net until his early 30s. As someone with dyslexia he found traditional methods hopeless until his accountant visually explained that gross was the number of fish overall and net were the ones caught in his net.

Make it your business to find out what is going on around you. Ask questions. Learn about things from a different perspective. If you work in one department make it a priority to talk to people in another area to understand what they are working on and why. Don't leave your school to educate your kids. Find out what they are studying and plan weekend activities to expose your children to new ways of learning the syllabus. Visit your local science museum and volunteer to help with your local adventure scout unit. Open your mind to learning new things at every conceivable opportunity.

Activity

Make a decision to find out about new things so that you are ahead of the curve. What 3 things have you heard about in your work or in the media that you could research?

Encourage healthy debate with colleagues about new approaches to problems. Bring together people with very different viewpoints to work on a project where they have to collaborate and encourage exploration of radical ideas to resolve issues.

Curiosity can be stimulated by organizing creative events where people can experiment and innovate without fear of failure.

What methods can you try to stimulate curiosity and ideas?

Focus on strengths not weaknesses

How many of us place more emphasis on weakness than strength? Imagine your teenage child came home with a school report card that said this:

Geography A

Spanish B

Physics C

Chemistry C

Art B

Mathematics B

English F

How many of us would focus on the fail in English first?

We are all wired differently and there is evidence to say that if we focus on the stronger subjects then we will have more confidence to tackle the weaker ones.

Of course it is important to learn from failure but we can get far more return for our time investment by maximizing strengths rather than minimizing weaknesses. A world class organization can only succeed if they are the best at what they do. They will never be more than average if they focus on something mediocre.

Activity

Write down your key strengths and weaknesses, then think of the wider opportunities and threats that challenge you in your professional and family life.

Strengths	Weaknesses
Opportunities	Threats

What steps can you take to maximize strengths and minimize weaknesses in the context of the opportunities and threats you have identified?

Write your own report card

How would you rate yourself in the following?
(A is highest to F for fail)

Professional/work skills	
Professional knowledge	
Work-life balance	
Family life	
Social life	
Health	
Wealth	
Happiness	
Future opportunities	

To turn this into a list of A's what changes would you have to make?

Based on your own life vision, what change would make the biggest impact?

Most people are about as happy as they make up their minds to be (Abraham Lincoln)

Excel in what you enjoy

We need to push ourselves beyond our current levels of ability in areas where we can excel so that we master a skill. To do that we need to identify what we enjoy as much as what we are good at, the two are usually the same.

Harrison Assessments have a behavioral theory based on 30 years of expertise in assessment technology that there is clear correlation between performance and enjoyment. When we enjoy an activity we get better at it and the opposite is also true so it is worth finding work that capitalizes on our strengths for a happy fulfilled life.

The only place where success comes before work is in the dictionary
(Donald Kendall)

Americans spend on average 34 hours per week watching television[10]. Add to that hours watching pre-recorded shows, playing computer/video games, internet searches, emailing and mobile phone use and imagine if we cut that time by half and invested the equivalent amount of time learning a new skill or developing a talent? How much more fulfilling would that be?

---

[10] Nielsen numbers survey 2012

If we want to be successful in the VUCA world we need to reduce time wasting TV etc. and increase activities that broaden our minds. This is not to say all TV is bad, far from it and some wonderfully educational programs can stimulate thinking but we need to discern for ourselves and our families the right balance.

Develop a creative mindset

*To be creative we must lose
our fear of being wrong
(Joseph Chilton Pearce)*

We need to make time to research and learn about new developments in industry, know what is going on politically, economically, socially, environmentally and be able to think about how to apply them to our own situations.

Innovation is putting new insights into action, trying something out. We all need to find ways of opening our minds to new opportunities which in turn will make us more inquisitive and resilient to change.

Practice in a safe environment

An accomplished presenter was asked where he learned his skill for communicating in such an entertaining and engaging way. His response was to tell the story of his early 20s where as a timid chef he wanted to find a way to develop the confidence to train others. He decided to go into a completely alien environment where no one knew him and volunteered to do a presentation on '10 ways to cook a chicken' to his local Women's Institute.

The ladies loved it and so did many other WI groups who invited him to speak at their meetings. Each presentation he grew in confidence and used humor to mask his nerves until it became second nature. He ended up travelling the length of Britain delivering his chicken talk to hundreds of women. This opened up new career options and he moved into a hospitality business where he became one of the best loved people managers of his company. Facing his fear of presenting head on, he transformed his career and life opportunities dramatically.

Questions/ Activities

1. What are the biggest challenges facing your industry or business?

2. Think of one new thing you could learn about that would challenge your thinking and give up a weeks-worth of TV "downtime" to research it.

3. Experiment with a new hobby, build something, paint a collage, grow a flower bed, write a story......something to engage your imagination and stimulate new thinking.

4. Find something going on in your community that you have never tried before where you have an under-developed talent, a singing group perhaps, a speaking group, running a tutorial for new business start-ups to hone your entrepreneurial skills and share your expertise.

5. Face a fear head-on by throwing yourself into a situation where you will have to deliver well outside your comfort zone. Be prepared to mess it up, dust yourself down and have another go.

Challenge views about money

Dan Pink in his TED talk on Motivation[11] refers to the three things that we need to ensure people are fulfilled and lead to better performance:

Autonomy – the desire to be self-directed

Mastery – the drive to keep improving at something important to us

Purpose – the sense that what we do produces something meaningful

This ground-breaking talk back in 2009 shattered the theory that money is a factor in motivation except in the most rudimentary of tasks. Pink tells us to pay people enough so that they aren't thinking about money which takes the issue off the table. Reward specialists who thrive on performance related pay and financially targeted objectives need to listen to Dan Pink.

Researchers into happiness[12] refer to the "hedonistic treadmill" where people soon adjust to their new wealth. They buy a more expensive house and then compare it to those of their new neighbors, raising their baseline expectation ever higher.

---

[11] Dan Pink TED talk on the Puzzle of Motivation 2009

[12] Lottery winners and accident victims, is happiness relative? Brickman P, Coates D, Janoff-Bulman R 1978

Studies of people who have won massive amounts of money on lotteries have concluded that once the initial excitement of being rich wears off the winner eventually reverts back to the same level of happiness they had before windfall and in some cases ends up wishing they hadn't won at all; so much for money as a motivator. In most cases the biggest pleasure came from giving it away and seeing it benefit the lives of others in practical ways. Many of the lottery winners experienced less pleasure from the day to day after their win and idealized their past.

Many of us have allowed consumerism to define our wants beyond our real needs. We strive to own things that display to ourselves and others that we are successful but under the surface there is a real danger that we get caught up in the cycle of always wanting, or even expecting more in spite of what we can actually afford.

Children are being bullied because they don't wear the right clothes label or have the most up to date cell phone. Many of us live beyond our means buying holidays, cars and so forth on credit which, instead of bringing happiness, can bring stress and financial disaster on our lives long after the excitement of the item has worn off.

Questions to ponder

How important is earning money to you?

_____

Does money define success for you and if it does why?

_____

Do you control your spending or does your spending control you? If you live beyond your means is it time to take a hard look at your spending and make plans to recover the situation, putting you in control?

Collaborate don't hoard

The VUCA world is becoming more and more collaborative. There are more ways than ever to benefit from the hard work of others through open–source software, websites, blogs, community groups, Wikipedia and so on. To maximize our potential we can gain far more by sharing expertise with others and forming strong networks with like-minded people who will benefit each other by pooling expertise. There has never been a time in history where expertise is so readily available.

Cross-promotion is a great way to attract new customers and it doesn't cost money. Find another company that complements your business and endorse them as they do the same for you. Large corporates like Pepsi and Doritos are a great example where they launched their "Fire and Ice" campaign in 2011 promoting each other's product. Both brands sold significantly more as a result.

Join business networks that encourage collaboration between companies to generate new business. Share expertise online and with professional groups that meet in person. Be prepared to give before you benefit. Taking the time to respond to questions can endorse your expertise and promote your business. Wikipedia provides a list of networks, numbers of members and the areas they focus on so you can be selective.

Make your work space collaborative by setting up offices that encourage interaction and innovation. Consider pooling resources with other businesses to economize on rent and

> *First you have to be visible in the community. You have to connect with people. It is not called net-sitting or net-eating. It is called Networking, you have to work at it*
> *(Dr Ivan Misner)*

sharing fees on services to bring overheads down.

Questions

1. What networks do you belong to now?

2. Are there other networks you could join that would be beneficial?

3. Find a business or organization that complements your work and explore ways to cross-promote.

4. Could you pool resources with another organization to mutual advantage?

The currency of real networking is not greed but generosity (Keith Ferrazzi)

Glance back- look ahead

Uncertainty can make us fearful of moving forward. Some people live most of their lives hankering for the "good old days" which have gone, if they ever existed. We do need to learn lessons from history and reflection is a key part of developing a VUCA mindset but it is important we keep that balanced with looking forward. Like the ploughman making furrows in the field, he needs to look far ahead to keep going straight and not get distracted by what is going on around him. Once in a while he needs to pause to check everything is working to plan and look back over his work.

We need to plan our time to check that we are going in the right direction, be sure we are 'ploughing the right field' and to include time for 'maintenance' of ourselves to succeed long term otherwise there is a real danger of investing lots of time in doing little of real substance.

Question

1. What are your plans for the next three months?

_____

2. How will you stay on track?

_____

3. How do you plan "maintenance/breaks" for yourself and your resources including vehicles, equipment and people you work with?

_____

Chapter Four
From Complexity to Clarity

*Strive for excellence not
perfection
(H Jackson Brown Jr)*

We need to know how to see through the haze of today so we make wise decisions about the future. The difference between managing and leading is that the manager organizes the team equipment, sets the start time, and gets everyone on their way: the leader is the one who says we are heading up the wrong mountain! Leaders are expected to make sense of the whole situation. In a VUCA world capable leaders grapple with the complexities they face and find new insight to lead through it.

No amount of disaster recovery planning can protect us from the new and varied threats that appear in our news bulletins daily: cyber-attacks, damaging social media controversy, political battles, media pressures, celebrity scandals, civil unrest, terrorism, theft, fire, natural disasters and so on.

We need to get used to feeling uncomfortable without losing our sense of integrity about the impact of such complexity, confusion and controversy.

The Consumer has power

Individuals are using social media to influence change. Consumer groups once had to resort to letters of complaint that lay dormant in an in-tray before a response was sent back. Today within a very short time one person can make a huge impact on the world.

Our reputation can turn on the basis of one posting on You Tube. Take the "United breaks guitars" protest song in 2009 by Dave Carroll as an example of what one consumer can do to the reputation of a massive company estimated to have cost them several million dollars when they refused to pay the cost of a replacement guitar.

More people have access to technology than ever before. The 2010-11 revolutions in Tunisia and Egypt were organized through social media campaigns in Africa and to generate international support as the message went global. Where historically supporters gathered in person to discuss grievances now people can organize action quickly via social media applications.

Mobile phone use is spreading rapidly across the African continent where people living in remote areas with no traditional phone lines are able to buy relatively cheap mobile technology for business and personal use. The Facebook page in support of the Egyptian revolution was joined by 80,000 online supporters in 2011 making it a key instrument in the campaign.

There is an inherent danger in the power of social media to influence people. As humans we tend to want to belong and the Gen Z's are the first true digital generation of our world so tuned in to technology that they see the world through screens almost as much as with their own eyes. We need to consider the implications of a teenager who has spent large parts of their childhood video gaming and communicating via social media.

Questions

How many hours on average do you and family members spend per week engaged with social media and what impact does that have positively or negatively?

How can you better utilize the benefits of social media?

What if any changes do you need to make?

Monitor, engage and be transparent; these have always been the keys to success in the digital space
(Dallas Lawrence)

Making sense of chaos

What we need in most cases is to break down the complexities of life into easy to digest pieces.

The confusion comes when we want to segment work, family, social and so on into separate compartments. Back in the 1960's – 70s it may have been possible to keep home and work totally separate with set meal times for the family, standard working hours and a social life removed from the home. The traditional family man worked 9 to 5, had dinner round a table with his family each evening and on weekends he may have enjoyed a round of golf or an hour in the pub with his friends. Work, family and social were compartmentalized and it was perfectly possible keep each part separate, with different behaviors applied to each.

Today our lives are so entwined it is much harder to work out where one thing starts and another finishes. We could be watching our son playing football, while chatting to another parent about the tennis, answering an email from work and at the same time returning a text to our spouse about what we plan for dinner.

We have become accustomed to being able to part-focus on several things at once and adept at juggling conflicting demands on our time. It has become quite normal for work calls late into the evening and emails peppered throughout a weekend.

> *Chaos in the world brings uneasiness,*
> *but it also allows opportunity for*
> *creativity and growth*
> *(Tom Barrett)*

Promote your own brand

Find smart ways to use the media to your advantage by creating your own stories. In 2013 Justin Bieber was running late for his own concert in London when Get Taxi capitalized on the opportunity and offered him a free ride to the venue, promoting their brand massively in the process.

Develop Blogs to share expertise and inform your customers and potential customers about what is going on in your profession.

Use sites such as survey monkey to research and provide compelling evidence to stimulate and create debate on local radio, TV and in whitepapers to demonstrate your expertise. Send a compelling press release to gain media coverage keeping the message simple using social media to make contact.

Handling a business crisis

Be ready to handle things when they go wrong. In a VUCA world we will all have testing challenges where things can spiral quickly out of control including product failures, financial crisis, high profile employee misconduct, accidents, protests, legal battles or injury/death where the media can be quick to make headlines out of the situation.

There is a real danger that our natural reaction to extreme pressure can make the situation worse if we allow the "flight or fight" response to take over our logic. Aggression, panic, paranoia, defensiveness and over reaction can turn a drama into a crisis.

We need to take action to minimize the impact of the situation by checking the facts so we can do the right thing quickly and regain control of the situation. To do this we need to address the media (both social and traditional) head on, establishing protocols on who can talk to the press. The way we handle the aftermath will be a testimony to the sort of business we are, long after the initial crisis has subsided.

When John Galliano was heard on video in a French bar making anti-Semitic remarks in the run up to the 2011/12 Paris fashion week, the head designer was fired by Christian Dior. Dior CEO Sidney Toledano made a strong statement saying "What has happened over the last week has been a terrible and wrenching ordeal for us all. It has been deeply painful to see the Dior name associated with the disgraceful statements attributed to the designer, however brilliant he may be", firmly establishing the company values and distancing themselves from Galliano.

Turning complexity into clarity

VUCA competent people will see through the situation and speak truth, no matter how unpopular that is. Like the boy in the story of the Emperor's new clothes we need to separate ourselves from the crowd and communicate common sense, exposing the truth where others stay silent.

Chapter Five
From Ambiguity to Agility

> *In these matters the only*
> *certain is that nothing is certain*
> *(Pliny the Elder 23AD-79AD)*

Dilemmas are problems without obvious answers. When we cannot make sense of a situation one reaction is to panic, rush in to make a decision without properly considering the facts and another is avoid it in the hope it will go away. Neither are VUCA competent responses.

Like the trapeze artist who focuses firmly ahead, perfectly poised and balanced, we need to stay in control and make considered steps that take us in the direction of our vision. Agility on the high wire requires a combination of balance, speed, strength and coordination, much the same as in our own VUCA competent lives. We also need to trust the high wire and the people who assembled it.

- We need to be **balanced** in our response to situations. We need to respond while maintaining a sense of perspective.
- Once decisions are made, they need to be taken **quickly**.

- We need to have the **strength of character** to take decisions and accept that sometimes we may get it wrong and then we need to have the integrity to accept responsibility no matter what.
- We have to **co-ordinate** our responses with others who need to know what is going on and how that impacts them, so communication is key.
- We need **confidence and trust** in the people around us.

Leadership agility

Leadership Agility is about being **focused** on the situation, **fast** in responding and **flexible** in our approach.

We need to have the tools necessary to work in a VUCA world and know how and when to use them. If we work across time zones, cultural and geographical barriers then we need to show people how to use technology and other tools to aid communication and understanding to remove the barriers.

VUCA leaders move knowledge quickly, sharing expertise across organizations so that people do not hoard skills. Collaboration on projects enables functional experts in one area to pass on key information and apply experience in a new context.

Enabling people to work flexibly is a key VUCA competent trait. Results only work environments (ROWE) are fairly new but they will grow in dominance. Major corporations are trialing the concept of giving employees freedom to work when they like as long as they deliver results in non-customer facing roles. Staff are paid for productivity and achievement instead of an hourly rate allowing people to strike their own balance between work and home, giving people autonomy to decide which meetings to attend, if any.

ROWE builds trust and autonomy. People enjoy the flexibility of being able to work whenever they want and value productivity measured by results, not face-time. Reports suggest that ROWE is self-policing because the workforce is highly protective of their new-found freedom so excuses are out and commitment is strong. In a world where our home, work and social lives are so inter-twined can we afford to ignore the benefits of ROWE?

Richard Branson has announced that he allows his 170 staff to take as much leave as they want, when they want and they do not need approval. The employee alone can decide how many days they feel they can take in line with their work commitments.

Question

Do you apply ROWE in your organization currently?

_____

What are the advantages and disadvantages of ROWE?

_____

_____

Learning from ambiguity

VUCA competent people take time to think about a situation after the event to capitalize on the knowledge and experience. If we jump from crisis to chaos without reflection we may miss out on key learning that can be used to enhance our development and in coaching others.

Many companies have the view that training consists of attending a course. In reality we know that the human brain retains a small percentage of "spoon-fed" learning, especially when the person is tired, distracted and bored. Memory retention in passive learning events can be as low as 10%.

When a person has to think for themselves and then coach another person, learning increases to as much as 90%.[13]

Learners retain around:

- 90% of what they learn when they teach someone else/ use immediately
- 75% of what they learn when they practice what they learned
- 50% of what they learn when engaged in a group discussion
- 30% of what they learn when they see a demonstration
- 20% of what they learn from audio-visual
- 10% of what they learn from reading
- 5% of what they learn from lecture

---

[13] The NLT institute in Bethel, Maine

Improv

One technique that is being used to stimulate creativity has been around for many decades in different guises.

Improvisation, or Improv is about creating action without planning. Spontaneous thoughts can spark innovation in a business or social context when people are free to contribute. Often Improv players tell a story, or go on a journey together as far as their imaginations take them.

Like most tools we need some boundaries to ensure it works well. Here are some guidelines:

- The first person introduces a short thought or idea.

- The next person responds with "yes…and…"accepting and building on the thought.

- Focused listening is crucial.

- Keep adding statements to the contributions made.

- Never block an idea or say no.

- Avoid asking questions, only make statements.

- Humor is great and encouraged.

Improv can be used as an ice breaker to energize a group or as a form of brainstorming innovative ideas.

Activity

Think of a situation where you can try out Improv as a way to brainstorm new ideas or as an energizer to get people out of their comfort zones and engaged in a team activity without a clear purpose.

Coaching network

One suggestion is to set up a network of people that are conversant with VUCA and meet to discuss VUCA challenges. Your group could meet monthly and each time a different member shares a VUCA challenge they are facing using the group as problem-solvers and idea generators. The Improv techniques above can add a fun and energy into the meeting and unlock innovative ideas that may not surface in a traditional brainstorm.

Asking for help

In reality all of us need help at some time and while we are usually happy to help others, asking for help is another matter, often because of pride. Identifying blockers and finding someone who can help makes us more effective and may even unlock solutions we haven't thought of.

Diet, exercise and sleep

We are bombarded with daily information on how to lose weight easily with some new fad and the only thing that is decreasing in size are our finances in paying for the new wonder solution and our willpower to continue, so in most cases we revert back to our old ways and move on to the next thing. In reality we also know that a permanent change to eating smaller portions of nutritious food, and exercising at least 3 times a week we will get most of us fitter and reduce excess fat. We need to break bad habits through real effort, and that takes VUCA competent agility and the mindset that goes with it.

> *Worrying about grey hair when your weigh's soaring out of control is like mowing your lawn while your house is on fire (Edward Ugel)*

A TV program broadcast in the UK in June 2014 researched 50 diets worldwide to find out which diet leads to better health and a longer life. Their conclusion was that Iceland's proliferation of fish and natural produce was the world's best cuisine, closely followed by the Mediterranean region where fresh fruit, vegetables, olive oil and nuts are common. Paradoxically the French diet was rated highly in spite of the proliferation of cheese and red meat. One factor that was common to all was the absence of processed food suggesting that good food in its natural state is better for all of us.

Exercise really does make a difference

If we are to cope with the increasing demands of life then it makes sense to maximize our opportunities by being as healthy as we can be, taking medical advice on what works best for us. A walk, swim, cycle or run will not only build stamina but it can also provide valuable reflection time.

As we have more demands placed on us we need to find smart ways of building exercise into our daily lives. Competitive people may enjoy the challenge of wearing a device to count each day's steps, compared with a colleague or family member. Perhaps set up a league with a group of friends to see who can clock up the most steps per month or even challenge yourself to beat your own targets.

Exercise can relieve pressure and give us a sense of wellbeing. Humans were not designed to sit for long periods at desks, followed by more hours slumped in front of a TV or games console. We were made to be active and our bodies need looking after.

Big sweeping life changes
really boil down to small
everyday decisions
(Ali Vincent)

Stress management

The chaos of modern life inevitably leads to stress for many people. Stress can start with too much pressure and can lead to emotional and physical symptoms usually when things get out of control.

A healthy busy life can move to stress quickly and our body's reaction to overload can reflect in our physical and mental well-being. Doctors' waiting rooms are full of people with conditions caused by stress and many of the symptoms mirror other physical or psychological conditions.

Key warning signs include feelings of helplessness, when everything seems hopeless, provoking feelings such as fear, anxiety, anger and mistrust.

We all operate with a basic level of stress in our lives but it is when it becomes prolonged that it needs attention before it spirals out of control. VUCA competent traits include being able to influence change and viewing life's challenges as opportunities rather than threats. We need to practice these skills to enable us to handle pressure and retain control of our lives. There are lots of techniques to use to maintain a healthy balance so that we stay on the safe side of pressure including exercise programs, meditation techniques and good support networks that if put in place ahead of time can help us to identify and prevent harmful stress and burnout.

Worry

VUCA competent people know that worry adds nothing to our lives, not even one minute, but it can certainly take a lot away. Worrying about something that may or may not happen in the future is a fruitless activity and can not only steal your joy in the present but it can affect your health in the long term. If you can do something about the thing that you are worried about, then do it. If no then accept that and move on.
We can probably all find 10 things in our lives to worry about right now and if all of them were resolved then another 10. If we allow ourselves to be preoccupied with things we cannot change then we will find the VUCA world increasingly hard to deal with.

Planned reflection

A busy life can be fun, exiting and build adrenalin as we jump from challenge to challenge but without reflection time it may be that we are going nowhere fast. A walk can release ideas and thoughts that would have stayed locked away. A break from your desk can stimulate the brain to re-evaluate what you are doing and a short conversation with a colleague may unlock a problem you have battled with for days. Take deliberate time-outs for reflection and do whatever works for you. Keep asking yourself is what I am doing now taking me towards or away from my vision?

Ideas to promote learning

Experiments with school boys with a lower than average reading age than their counterpart girls found that when you took the boys outside for an adventure, making dens and climbing trees, they were much more open to reading. If you are frustrated with traditional learning methods break the mold and change your environment, it may be exactly what you need to unlock a new skill.

Listen to webinars while doing household chores. Instead of watching TV, play a TED talk as you make dinner, do the ironing or clean the house. Not only will it lighten the load while you work, it will fill your head with thoughts and ideas to use later.

Attend seminars and events that will enable you to meet like-minded people. Breakfast seminars may not sound so appealing if you are rushing to work but invariably the time invested is worth the effort.

Volunteer for something new that will enable you to improve a skill. If you want to learn more about finance but don't have the opportunity at work, try helping a local charity keep their accounts in order, using the help of others where needed. If you want to improve your sales technique spend a few Saturday mornings running a charity stall for a worthwhile cause, perfecting your selling ability and getting to know new people in the community.

*If you don't risk anything, you risk
even more
(Erica Jong)*

VUCA Competency Model

Using Harrison Assessments toolkit we have produced a behavioural competency assessment profile to objectively assess the strengths and development needs to both survive and succeed in the VUCA world. Each of the four essential traits listed below is made up of many competencies which are weighted in terms of essential requirements.

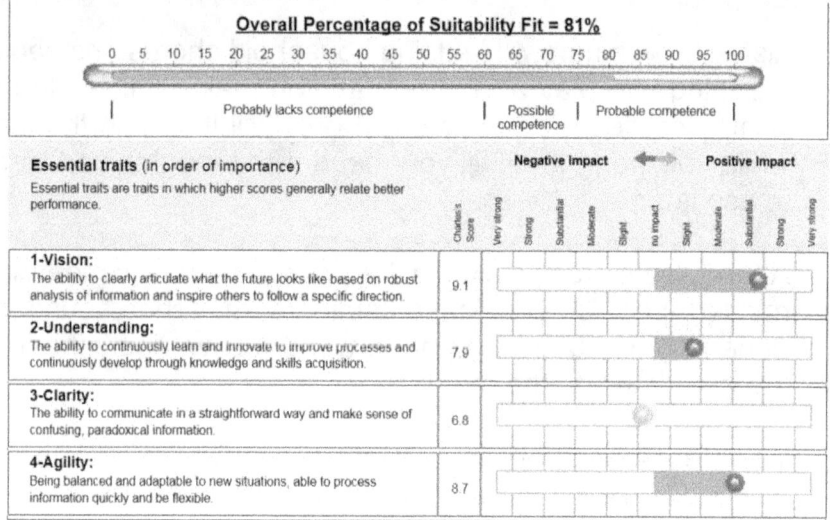

In this example, we are able to measure the four VUCA competent areas; Vision, Understanding, Clarity and Agility. We see that this person needs to develop in the area of clarity.

We are then able to drill down and identify the specific competencies requiring focus.

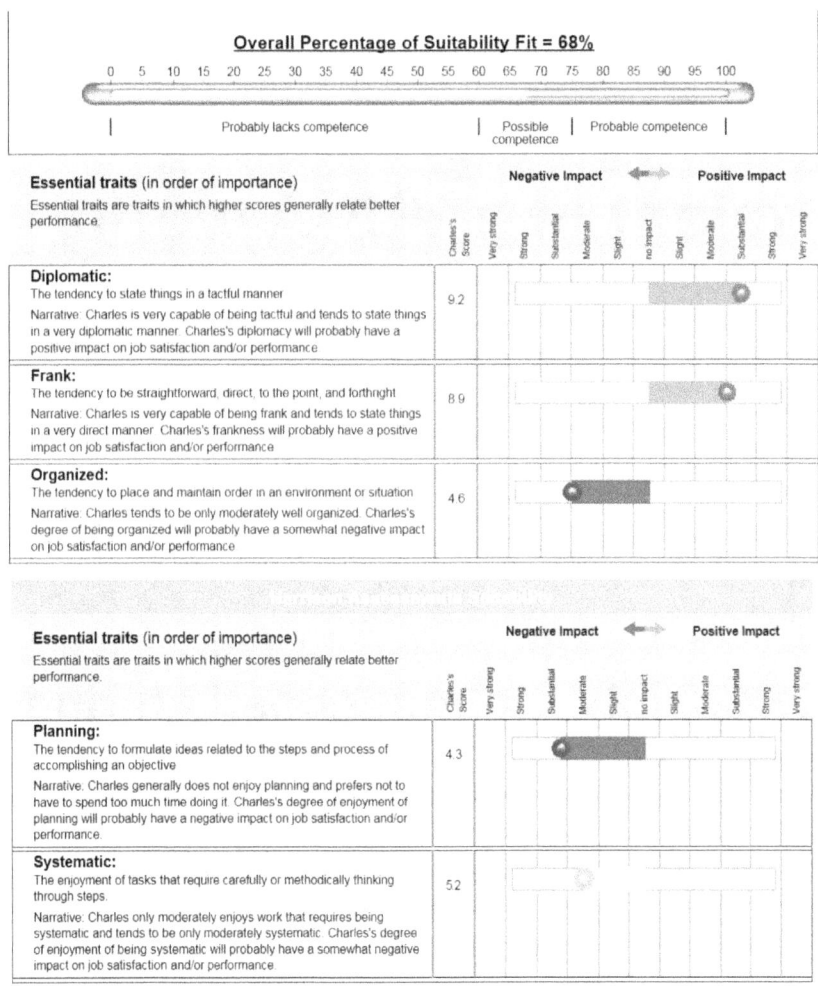

From the above we can clearly see that this person needs to develop their planning and organizing ability as well as becoming more systematic and a further report can be used to produce a development plan to address these areas.

Chapter Six
Hiring and retaining talent in a VUCA world

There is something that is much more scarce, something rarer than ability. It is the ability to recognize ability
(Robert Half)

Possibly the most costly hiring mistake?

In 2014 Facebook bought What's App for $19bn appointing founders Brian Acton and Jan Koum to their Board, paying Acton close to $3bn in stock and cash and Koum around $6bn as part of the acquisition deal. In 2009, Brian and Jan applied to Facebook but were turned down by their recruiters, so that hiring decision arguably cost Facebook $9bn or even $19bn if you include the market value of the product. The question we need to ask is why Facebook let these visionary engineers slip through their recruitment net 5 years earlier. Brian Acton even posted on his Facebook account at the point he was rejected: "Facebook turned me down. It was a great opportunity to connect with some fantastic people. Looking forward to life's next adventure". Khoum applied shortly after and suffered the same fate.

Employers may not make mistakes that run into billions but recruitment processes are rejecting good candidates and worse still selecting wrong people for their organizations at great cost.

Why does hiring fail?

The answer is our over reliance on interviews which in most cases are biased towards replicating the traits of the person interviewing. Even with a structured competency based interview, we allow subjective things to get in the way. It is estimated that the average CV gets about 30 seconds of the recruiters time before they make it to the "yes" "no" or "possible" file and we make our minds up about a candidate at interview within minutes, even seconds of them walking into the room.

At Executive levels remember 80% of CEOs of the 2500 world's biggest organizations are based in their home country and only 35% have worked in different cultures or geographies so is it any wonder that most of our senior managers hire people who behave and in some cases even look just like them. Companies who hire people based on the sheer force of their personality at interview will miss out on great candidates that will end up working for someone else – or maybe set up as a competitor.

Executive recruitment companies tout the same select network of candidates round the revolving door of businesses from one organization to the next making money no matter whether a far better candidate was ignored in the process, using little more than interviews and CVs sifted for key words to verify they are right for the job.

Hiring people is a risk. The cost of a bad executive hire is estimated to be between 3 and 5 times their annual salary. In a global war for talent finding tomorrow's leaders today should not be left to chance. We need to identify people who truly exhibit VUCA competent traits and they may not come from the traditional network of candidates.

How do you hire VUCA competent people?

Put simply to make sure you hire people with VUCA competent traits use robust assessment tools such as Harrison Assessments (HA) to sift candidates based on job specific criteria and VUCA traits.

Harrison Assessments has over 20 years of performance research and expertise to measure essential and desirable competencies that are specific to your roles and organization rather than a generic set of traits.

This unique assessment technology predicts job success far higher than structured interviews because it reveals behavioral skills and versatility. Paradox Technology™ identifies the relationship between traits for example diplomatic and frank. For detailed information go to **www.vucaready.com**

Right people, right place, right time

VUCA competent hiring is based on the principle that people are not your most important asset; the right people are[14]. Most of us know the headache of having to manage out a perfectly nice person who simply can't or sometimes won't do their job. We need to first find the right people and then make sure we put them in the right roles at the right time for the business.

In his book, Good to Great, Jim Collins talks about getting the right people on the bus and making sure they are sitting in the right seats before you set off on your journey to become a great company. There is no point starting down the road if the people with you are not passionately committed to what you are doing and why.

If you put a pot on your stove but the stove is not turned on, your soup will stay cold no matter how wonderful the cooking device looked in the saleroom. If you want to be a truly great organization you have got to make sure the people you hire are "turned on" to your business so that together you achieve great results. If you hire or work with people who do not have the potential or the inclination to move with you as you take on the challenges of the VUCA world they will undermine and possibly prevent success.

---

[14] Taken from Jim Collins' book Good to Great

The HA assessment process can be used to tell you which candidates most closely match the VUCA behavioral traits for hiring new people, internal promotion and talent development. A full profile will give you development needs for the position you are hiring for which will give you some very helpful areas to probe in more detail during the recruitment process.

The report can also tell you how to attract the candidate which will be useful if you are keen to recruit and the person is undecided on whether to join your organization.

Review new hires straight away

When you recruit someone, make sure you meet with them after a few days to find out how they are getting on. This will flag any induction issues early. In addition ask them for feedback on the hiring process so that you can fine tune and improve how you market to candidates. Finally ask them for insights into their former company, what worked well and from their understanding of your organization what ideas do they bring with them.

Questions

Why does a strong candidate in company A fail to perform in company B?

What forms of recruitment do you use to hire new people and how well do they predict high performance in the new role?

What hiring mistakes can you think of from the past and how could they have been avoided?

Retaining Talent

There is no business like show business but there are several businesses like accounting (David Letterman)

When you have talented people the biggest challenge is to retain them.

Harrison Assessments can also show you what you need to do to retain your key VUCA talented people. If someone has completed the assessment you will be able to obtain a report showing what is important to them in terms of personal motivation in their career and personal life.

You will see whether the need to work for a strong leader outweighs salary. Is it career progression or growth and development within a role that is important?

Whatever it is, know what it is and make sure you work on a plan to keep them.

If all else fails and they move on, keep contact with them through networks, collaborative opportunities, social media etc. and looking ahead it may be that you can benefit even more from them returning to your business wiser than before and having worked for the competition!

Solutions to retain talent

Tailor ways to retain talent to the individual. Here are some ideas to consider depending on their VUCA profile:

Coach/mentor

Identify a strong role model prepared to invest time in building a coaching relationship. If your organization is small it may work better to find someone externally. Reciprocal arrangements can be mutually beneficial where you coach a person from another business in exchange for one of their leaders coaching someone working for you.

Lateral moves

Sideways moves are often under-rated as we expect to climb up the ladder but they can be highly beneficial longer term. A senior finance manager may grow potential faster after a move into a marketing role and an HR professional may learn more about the business after a stint working in a customer facing role.

Grow job content

Give highly talented people more responsibility and autonomy in the job they are in. Consider merging two roles together to add substance to a role. Think objectively about new ways to utilize their skills in the business by adding project and development activities that challenge their thinking and grow experience.

Overseas secondment

Remembering 65% of the CEOs of the world's 2500 largest organizations have never experienced working internationally, imagine how powerful it would be to undertake an overseas secondment to work with a supplier or another part of your business as part of a career development plan. Again reciprocal agreements can work well for both parties.

Flexible options

Flexible working allows for personal interests to be accommodated and retains quality people. People who work in a ROWE environment on the whole are reluctant to leave because they value the freedom to work the hours that best suit their circumstances. Companies that stick rigidly to rules about hours will lose goodwill and lose staff at a much higher rate than their competitors.

Chapter Seven
Leadership and personal development in a VUCA world

*Great ability develops and
reveals itself increasingly with
every new assignment
(Baltasar Gracian)*

It doesn't matter if we are a small collaborative consultancy or the CEO of a massive enterprise, we are all operating in the same VUCA world and need to develop our VUCA competency traits both to succeed and lead. Many of us state that we treat people the way we like to be treated or manage others like we want to be managed. There is a real danger in this.

We are all different, even siblings brought up in the same family, going to the same school, watching the same TV programs can respond very differently to the same stimuli. One child may be petrified of spiders and the other enjoy dangling them in front of their faces to make them squirm. Even twins can have very different characteristics in spite of being born and growing up together.

If this is true when the social and environmental factors are more or less equal then it is obvious that a group of people from varied backgrounds will have very different reactions to what is going on around them. A new computer system to process orders can fill one person with dread, another with excitement and the bore the third who doesn't care as long as the job gets done.

The skill of a leader is to possess a range of competencies so that they can move the organization forward while bringing the best out of the people around them. In the VUCA world flexibility is far more necessary than control. We need the agility to be able to react quickly and make 180° changes if necessary and we can only do that if the team are on side and equally committed to adding real value to the organization.

The people we put in charge of our teams make a massive difference and where there are numbers of employees the multiplier effect can be huge. It is said that we join an organization and leave a manager. Invariably the main reasons cited when people resign from organizations are lack of career opportunities and issues with their manager. Money may be a factor but it is rarely a reason in isolation unless pay rates are well below the market. A good people manager can leverage high performance in the team well above expectations, differentiating them from others by building a sustainable, value added, culture that competitors will struggle to copy.

Ability will never catch up with
the demand for it
(Malcolm Forbes)

We need to objectively assess ourselves against VUCA competencies to know where we are now. Use Harrison Assessments (HA) to identify VUCA strengths and development areas, find ways to maximize talents and grow in areas of natural ability. Our own HA VUCA profile will give us an objective assessment of where we are in terms of strengths and will show us areas that can be improved. Our development plan needs to maximize strengths as much as focusing on the weaker areas that would benefit improvement.

Activity

Look at areas for development and weigh up the effort v reward of spending time improving in those areas.

Quick ways of getting up to speed

- Get someone else to do it – in business outsource parts of your process to someone better in that area. Don't try to be the best at everything, focus on what you are good at.
- Pay someone to do your marketing for you if that is not your talent.
- Use networking to grow ideas and identify ways to fill skill gaps.
- Collaborate with people who have skills in areas you can benefit from and vice versa.

Find a mentor

One of the fastest ways to manage your career is to find a mentor already successful in his or her field and ask them to meet with you regularly to discuss everything from long term career goals to your approach on a particular piece of work. Agility is learning from people around you and a strong leadership role model can provide insight into why they made certain decisions and how you can apply them. The mentor will benefit too because, in relaying things to you, they are also reviewing and learning themselves.

You may be a leader in your field but there are always benefits of having a good coach or mentor even when you are at the top of your game like Andre Agassi, one of the world's best tennis players. Agassi explained that "tennis requires subtle adjustments crucial to winning and my coach, Gill, is the best at making them. The older I get the more valuable he becomes."

Activity

Produce your own development plan identifying:

- Areas to work on
- Resources you need
- People who can help you
- Dates for review
- Timescales for achievement of plans

Chapter Eight
Your VUCA success plan
guaranteed!

*A positive attitude may not
solve all your problems, but it
will annoy enough people to
make it worth the effort
(Henry Albright)*

Our future is VUCA whether we want it or not. We can put this book back on the shelf, run away from the VUCA world and hope it will go away, or we can take meaningful steps towards our goals in every aspect of our lives. The decision is truly ours.

The story goes that one day a wise old man and his granddaughter were sitting in their front garden when a passer-by stopped to enquire, "What is this neighborhood like?"

"What is the neighborhood like where you live now"? asked the old man.

"Awful said the visitor, "everyone gossips about each other and no one is prepared to help out". "Well you will find very much the same here" said the old man.

A little while later another person stopped by and asked "What is this neighborhood like?"

The old man answered. "What is the neighborhood like where you live now"?

The visitor said: "Wonderful, everyone looks out for each other and it is so friendly"

"Well you will find very much the same here" said the wise old man.

As the wise man inferred the world is pretty much as you view it. We can all choose to have a "half-full or half-empty" attitude to it.

Don't let fear take over

The 18, 40, 60 rule

When you are 18 you will worry about what other people are saying about you.

When you are 40 you will stop worrying about what others are saying about you.

When you are 60 you will realize that they weren't talking about you in the first place.

Many of us worry about things that have no real importance in our lives. Fear is a natural response that serves to increase our heart rate to allow us to get away from something dangerous or triggers the fight response to attack if we are trapped.

In 1898 DC Robertson from Scotland was running a coffee plantation in Malawi and he decided to take an evening cycle on a very uneven new road. At one point he got off to push his bike up a slope when he heard something large behind him which turned out to be an adult lion. He jumped back on the bike and pedaled for his life at speeds he didn't know he was capable of, damaging the front fork as he turned into an open culvert and was flung high out of the saddle but somehow managed to stay on. Eventually the lion gave up chasing him and he got away.

Clearly the fight or flight responses are helpful if a dangerous wild animal is about to attack but they aren't useful reactions in a business or social context.

Fear is an emotion that can blind us from the reality of a situation where we should be asking ourselves: "what is the worst that can happen". We can waste so many precious life opportunities worrying about things that have no impact on us or allowing irrational fear to prevent us from trying something new.

Activity

Name something you have always wanted to try but haven't because of fear?

What day to day tasks do you avoid because of misplaced fear?

Make a decision now to do something that you don't want to do, but know it would be good for you to do, with a time and date to achieve it by:

Integrity

Actions lie louder than words
(Carolyn Wells)

VUCA competent people need to be transparent and trustworthy. Our actions need to mirror our words and if they don't we will be recognized quickly as frauds. Companies that survive now by taking advantage of loopholes or offer substandard service will be exposed more and more by consumers who will not accept being overcharged or lied to by a business. Social media has already "outed" many fly-by-night practices and the power of the customer to influence this is increasing.

As the world gets more complex there will be opportunities for fraudulent practice but digital technology is getting better at tracking people and reputations will be won or lost on the people we associate ourselves with and the business practices we keep. In a survey of employers[15], honesty and trustworthy were rated as numbers 1 and 2 of a list of 20 things employers really want in their employees and character traits were valued far more than skills.

A strong positive mental attitude will create more miracles than any wonder drug (Patricia Neal)

Your life vision

If you haven't produced your vision statement do it now. Take deliberate time out from the day to day and reflect on where you want to be 10 years from now.

Listen to successful people who have achieved their goals and read about how they did it. Invariably most of the "good luck" will have come from hard work and concerted effort combined with a clear plan for their future.

---

[15] Survey by REED detailed in Put your Mindset to Work by James Reed

Glance back and learn from the past but focus most of your attention on maximizing your future potential by looking ahead at where you want to be and making every day count towards your goals.

Don't let another day, week, month, year or even decade go by without taking stock of where you are against where you want to be.

Review your life vision and take practical steps to plan how you will fulfill it.

Find someone you trust to act as a mentor to help you to stay on track.

Your life purpose

> *Happiness lies not in the mere possession of money. It lies in the joy of achievement, in the thrill of creative effort*
> *(Franklin D Roosevelt)*

Ask yourself every day if what you are doing is taking you towards or away from your vision.

At the end of each month instead of merely compiling your expenses, allocate time to make sure you are on track long term to achieve your vision by setting short, medium and long term goals. If you have let that month go by without making key changes then left to chance the same will happen next month and before you know it, a year and even a decade will pass without moving towards your vision.

Activity

Set a diary appointment at the end of each month to review progress against your life goals and vision. Give yourself permission to get away from the day to day and build reflection time somewhere you cannot be disturbed.

Look at your progress for the month and recognize success. Review things that you can improve on.

Build next month's plan.

A stitch in time saves nine

Get focused

Many of us will have read books on time management, maybe even attended a seminar. There are some great techniques available and we need to find methods that work for us. In a VUCA world we will have to be ruthlessly well organized so that we have the capacity and freedom to innovate and make decisions away from the chaos of modern living.

We will need good routines and habits that keep us focused on the important. Every night we will need to write a list of the things we have to do the next day and put fool-proof reminders in place such as phone alarms, diary reminders or notes to make sure they cannot be forgotten as we are distracted with new demands on our time.

Routines can take the stress out of every day issues such as arriving at a meeting early and remembering to switch off the ring tone on your phone. Then immediately after a meeting taking a couple of minutes to place any actions you have agreed to into your diary with a date and time attached and to remember to switch your phone back on again!

Good routines can keep us calm in a crisis. If we are running late then it is great to have the details of the person we are meeting logged in our diary to call without having to spend time searching for them.

Being early can not only take the pressure off, but it can be valuable reflection time ahead of an event to ensure you know what you want to achieve out of it.

Filter out the distractions

Imagine you are standing near a busy highway with traffic roaring past at high speed. Nearby is a farm field full of wildlife, birds in the hedgerows and bees gathering pollen from the wild flowers. Perhaps you are oblivious to the beauty of the field because all you can hear is the domination of the road noise. As a VUCA competent person you will be able to block out the traffic and discern the wider environment around you as you filter out the chaos of everyday life.

We know that the urgent is often exciting and there is also the short term feeling of success when solve a problem but how often do we intervene when we should stand back and allow others, possible more junior to take action? To add real value to an organization we have to focus on the things that build long term value and create sustainable advantage against the competition and we cannot do that if we are operating primarily in the here and now.

Question

What are the distractions that prevent you from focusing on the bigger picture?

Remove Barriers

Get into the habit of making time for important things by resolving trivial things quickly. You may have a pile somewhere in your house of things that need attention, some unwanted clothing to give to the charity shop, an electrical item that needs a new plug or a bicycle that needs repairing, for example. The items can often stay in the same state for months, if not years without attention. Not only is this cluttering up our house, but it is also cluttering up your mind.

Every time you pass the broken bike it puts failure into your mind. You have allowed this item to stay in this state and have wasted time in failing to do something about it. Imagine instead that the day the bike broke down, you loaded it onto your bike rack and drove it to the cycle repair shop having it restored for your pleasure one week later, along with the bag of clothes to donate the charity shop at the same time. Now that not only gives you a feeling of satisfaction but it also puts you in control.

We can apply these principles to all aspects of our lives. Handle emails only once. Set up systems to log "next actions" to move complex things forward and "waiting for" items when others need to get back to you. Make sure you build checks so that you keep track of important things and set up good routines to group tasks efficiently. Filter out distractions by switching off from the day to day when you need to focus on the things that move you forward.

Activity

Evaluate the way you handle your emails. Do important ones get missed? Do you read the same message more than once? Are there improvements you can make?

Eat your frogs first

Mark Twain joked that if you eat a frog first thing every day you will go through the day knowing nothing worse can happen. Make a habit of eating your "frogs" first and that will give you a sense of achievement that you can build on for the rest of the day. If there is a job that fills you with dread, the worst thing you can do is put it off. That will increase your resistance and play on your mind (and potentially disturb your sleep) until it is done. If you need to break it down, use the 15 minute rule – set an alarm for 15 minutes and make a start. The chances are once you have begun you will continue and if not set your alarm 15 minutes every day until it is behind you.

Activity

What items do I need to give a 15 minute rule to and when will I start them?

Look back over the activities and questions in the book. Are there any still to complete?

What are the things that you still need to address to enable your long term vision to become reality?

_____

Who can help you to address any barriers to success?

_____

What have you learned from *Are you VUCA ready?*

_____

How can you help others to benefit from your learning?

_____

Who can you recommend this workbook to?

_____

Are you VUCA ready?

- ✓ You have read the book, completed the exercises.

- ✓ Your life vision is written, you are making the changes necessary to achieve it.

- ✓ You are a visionary and can articulate future plans to others.

- ✓ You have built effective organization into your day.

- ✓ You are able to filter out distractions in your environment and see the way ahead.

- ✓ You create, innovate and experiment with new ideas.

- ✓ You can communicate effectively - people understand you.

- ✓ Collaboration, sharing and networking are part of your daily life.

- ✓ You strive for results and persevere no matter what obstacles you face.

- ✓ You can analyze information and use intuition to solve complex problems.

- ✓ You can energize and motivate other people towards their goals.

- ✓ You love learning and always seek to know more.

So to sum up with a final sentence…

If you want to be VUCA ready forget excuses and

Just Do IT!

And if you have not already done so, email us for your special discounted assessment which includes feedback on your profile for only £25+VAT. Full details can be found on www.vucaready.com and we would love to hear from you about your VUCA experiences, thoughts and ideas.

Charles@talentfactor.co.uk
Jayne@hroptions.co.uk

www.ingramcontent.com/pod-product-compliance
Lightning Source LLC
Chambersburg PA
CBHW051338170526
45166CB00002B/867